Conversations That Transition to Community

Lisa K. Smith and Maggie Rogers

© 2022 Lisa K. Smith and Maggie Rogers

All rights reserved. No part of this book may be used or reproduced in any manner whatsoever without permission from the publisher, except in the case of brief quotations embodied in critical articles and reviews.

Book design by Patricia Oman

ISBN-13: 978-1-942885-87-0

- Community 3
- Identity 15
- Connection 31
- Creation 51
- Engagement 65

Field Book   Primary source documents that describe the events leading up to and including the collection of specimens or observations during field research. Field notes can take many forms depending on the information needs of the collector.*

ABOUT THIS BOOK

 Pause what you are doing and come together to create a **circle**.

 **Check-in** presents an intentionally selected question for us to respond to in the group. **Check-out** occurs outside of the group, in preparation for our next discussion.

 **Compass** indicates we will work together to bring ideas to the surface that contribute to developing skills, knowledge, and self-awareness. Capturing what arises out of our conversations will give you a reference point for on-going learning.

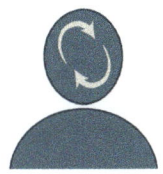 Asks you to **reflect** quietly and record your thoughts.

* "The Field Book Project," Smithsonian National Museum of Natural History. naturalhistory.si.edu.

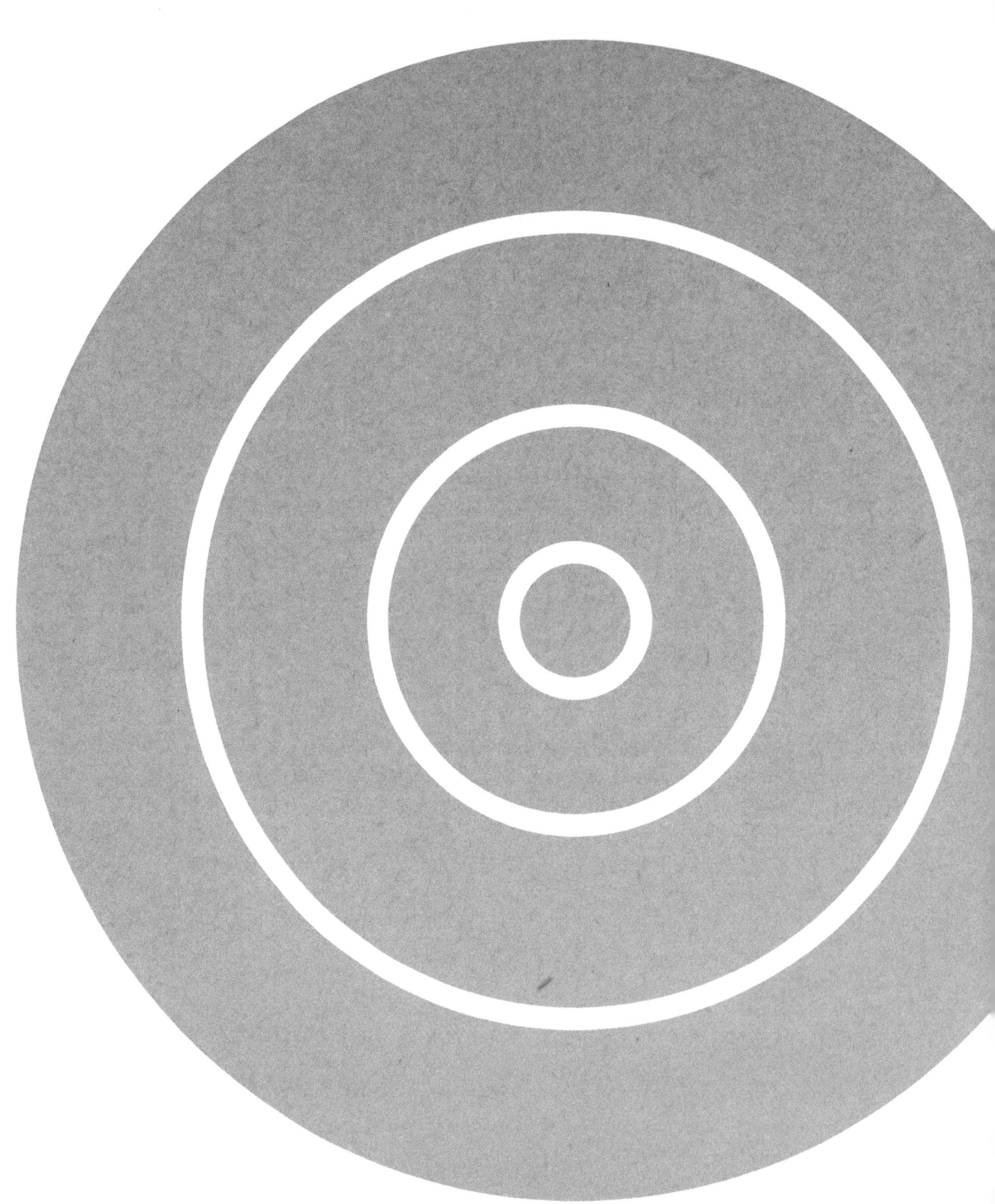

Lisa's Pop-up Camper Story

A few years ago, my friends and I went in together on an older model pop-up camper that serves us well for mini-adventures throughout the summer. On a recent trip to a campground we had not visited before, we were pleased with many things when we arrived. The lake was large, and we were surrounded by stately trees and lush vegetation. There was a marina that sold ice, kayaks were ready to hit the water, and there were hiking trails should we feel motivated to explore them.

After setting up the camper, we arranged chairs around the fire pit and settled into what we always anticipate will be a satisfying experience. This time, we realized that the cute little beach area just over the rise was a busy place where someone was blasting some *very* loud music. We also realized that in our line of vision was a *very* large boat parked on the edge of our site. Did I mention that the music was *very* loud and the boat (and its truck) were *very* large?

They were.

I could feel my shoulders tense, my face tighten into "not happy," and my mind throw out judgment about these invaders of my space and my peace.

Then, I sat *very* still and had myself a little revelation.

These excursions with our cute little camper are forays into temporary settlements. There are usually some written campground rules about fires and trash and dog poop, but we all also carry with us unwritten rules that reflect what we know about being in community with others. While I wouldn't turn my music up *very* loud or park my *very* big boat (if I had one) right at the edge of someone else's space, those are the rules *I* carry with me. Obviously, other people have different unwritten rules.

In this temporary blending of diverse ideas and ways of being, I had a choice to make. I could let these details about what others bring with them ruin my experience or I could recognize that I was sharing communal space and make room for different ways of hanging out in the world together and make community work.

As soon as I made my choice, I moved my chair a little to the left to get a better view of the lake and started tapping my foot to an unfamiliar beat. It was a great weekend.

In this section you will:

- Reflect on past experiences of community and make connections to the present
- Practice the principles of calling a dialogic circle
- Experience the various roles of circle practice
- Create agreements of circle and of community

BASIC GUIDELINES FOR CALLING A CIRCLE

This space will hold "Basic Guidelines for Calling a Circle," located at www.thecircleway.net. (Select Resources → Guidelines → Language of Choice.)

Glue page 1 of "Basic Guidelines for Calling a Circle" here.

Glue page 2 of "Basic Guidelines for Calling a Circle" here.

CIRCLE WAY
www.thecircleway.net

MAIN ROLES

GUARDIAN
Protects the energy and good will of the circle by calling for pauses. Tends to the beginning and end of discussions via a "vibe check."

KEEPER
Keeps the circle focused by asking questions such as: What question calls us together? What is currently in the center? What's next?

SCRIBE
Records experiences and discussions and serves as the circle historian. Gathers and harvests moments for the circle's collective memory.

GUIDELINES

- Recognize that the Guardian has the floor.
- Offer your name.
- Respond to the question posed, as you are able. If you are not ready to answer, you may pass and the circle will return to you.
- Clap your hands twice to acknowledge that the speaker has been heard.
- Listen with curiosity and compassion.

SETTING AGREEMENTS

As a group, determine the guidelines you will hold to while in circle with each other and in the community generally.

DATE:

AGREEMENTS OF CIRCLE:

AGREEMENTS OF COMMUNITY:

DATE REVISITED:

DATE REVISITED:

DATE REVISITED:

CHECK IN

In small groups, discuss what showed up in your conversation about agreements. How do you feel about it? What's next for this community?

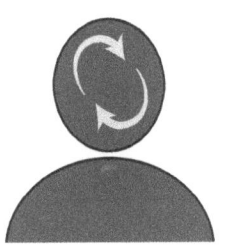

REFLECTION QUESTION

How have you embodied each role of circle in your own experiences? How will you help to create community in the future?

10   Community

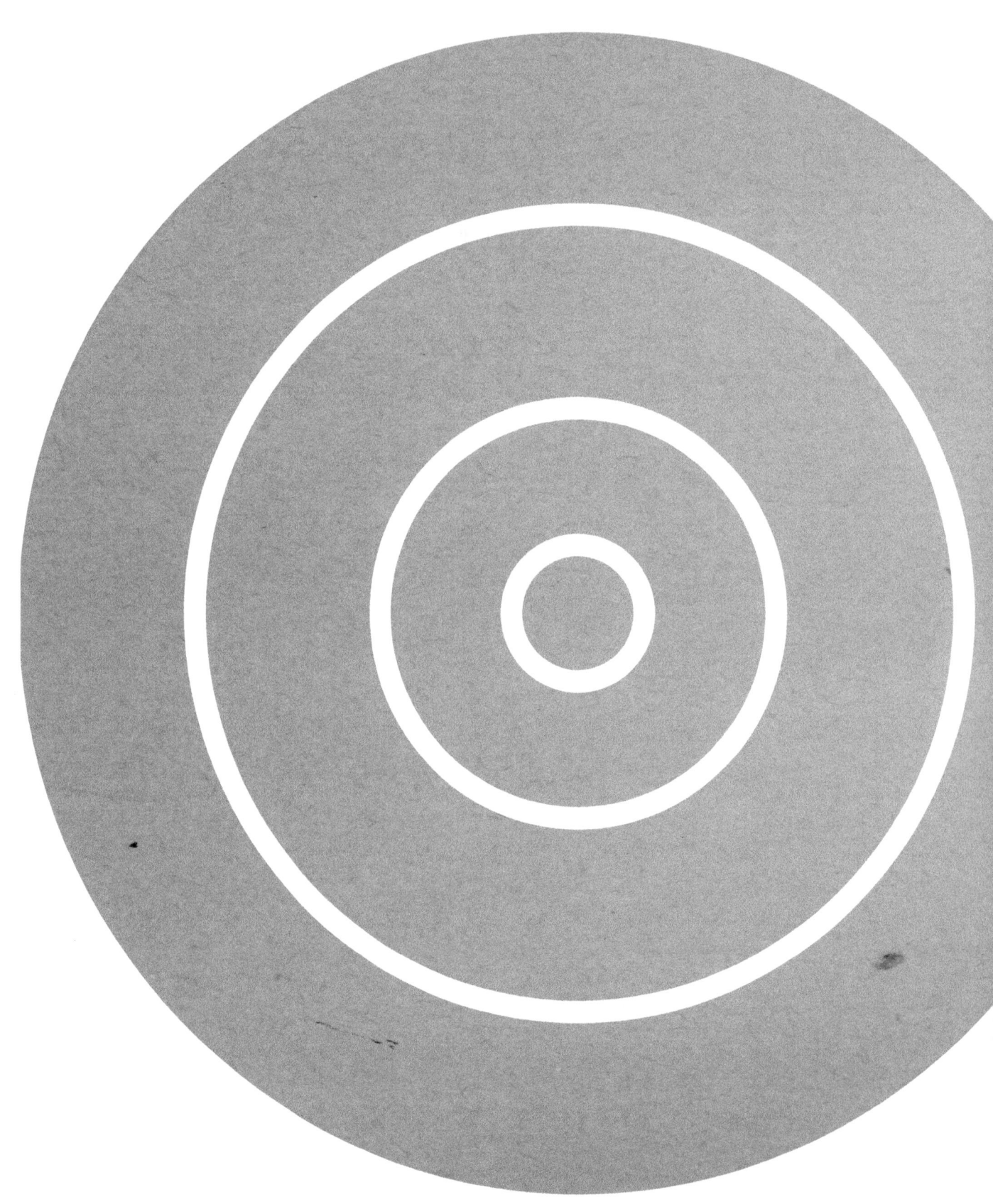

Lisa's Beet Story

Back in 1968, my parents lived on a farm and made do on a shoestring budget. Slowly making the old farmhouse their own, my mother spent some of her precious funds to paint the kitchen and dining room a lovely shade of buttercream yellow…

My sister and I both love to travel. When we travel, we both bring little parts of the experience back and incorporate them into our own routines. A few years ago, we went to lunch after one of her adventures and she was telling me about a little restaurant she found that served a salad with a unique blend of ingredients. Listing off things such as pumpkin seeds, goat cheese, and various summer vegetables, she had me hooked until she noted, "oh, yeah! Raw, shredded beets!" and I cringed and visibly and clearly expressed my disgust.

Surprised, she asked why I had such adverse feelings for beets when I consumed every other vegetable she could imagine? Out came the reminder about the legendary story of me in a high chair and mother's pride and joy—freshly painted, buttercream yellow walls—and the beets she fed me for the first time. I didn't like those beets, and the lovely yellow wall just over my mother's right shoulder paid the price. And had to be repainted. My feelings about beets became the stuff of family legend.

"When was the last time you tried beets?"

Long pause.

"1968"

It was at that exact moment my mind exploded just a little bit. Why was I clinging to this story about myself? What other stories were people telling about me, to me, that I was clinging to as if they were absolutely true? Were they?

I tried beets. Shredded raw on a salad, pickled from a jar, dried into chips, roasted and served warm with a little butter … and I loved them in every form. I started buying them at the farmers market until I could make room for them in my garden.

What stories do we hear told that we take on ourselves as The Truth? Are they?

Times of transition are times to reassess the narrative of our lived experience and check in: Was this me? Is it still me? Was it never me? Who am I now? What do I aspire to as I take these forward steps into a space that feels new to me?

I let go of that beet story and so many more since then. Let them go and made room for new stories to replace them.

Identity

In this section you will:

- Reflect on the factors that form identity
- Collaborate in forming inclusive community
- Practice engaged and active listening
- Explore lived experiences through a process of inquiry

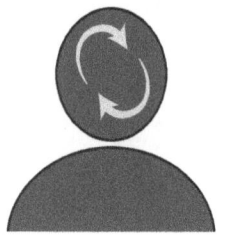

HUMAN IDENTITIES

What or who has influenced you?

_____   _____   _____
_____   _____   _____
_____   _____   _____
_____   _____   _____

Fill this circle with the ways you identify as a human.

16   Identity

LIKENESSES AND DIFFERENCES

In small groups, each person choose a blue circle and add attributes that make them unique. In the yellow circle, add attributes the group members share.

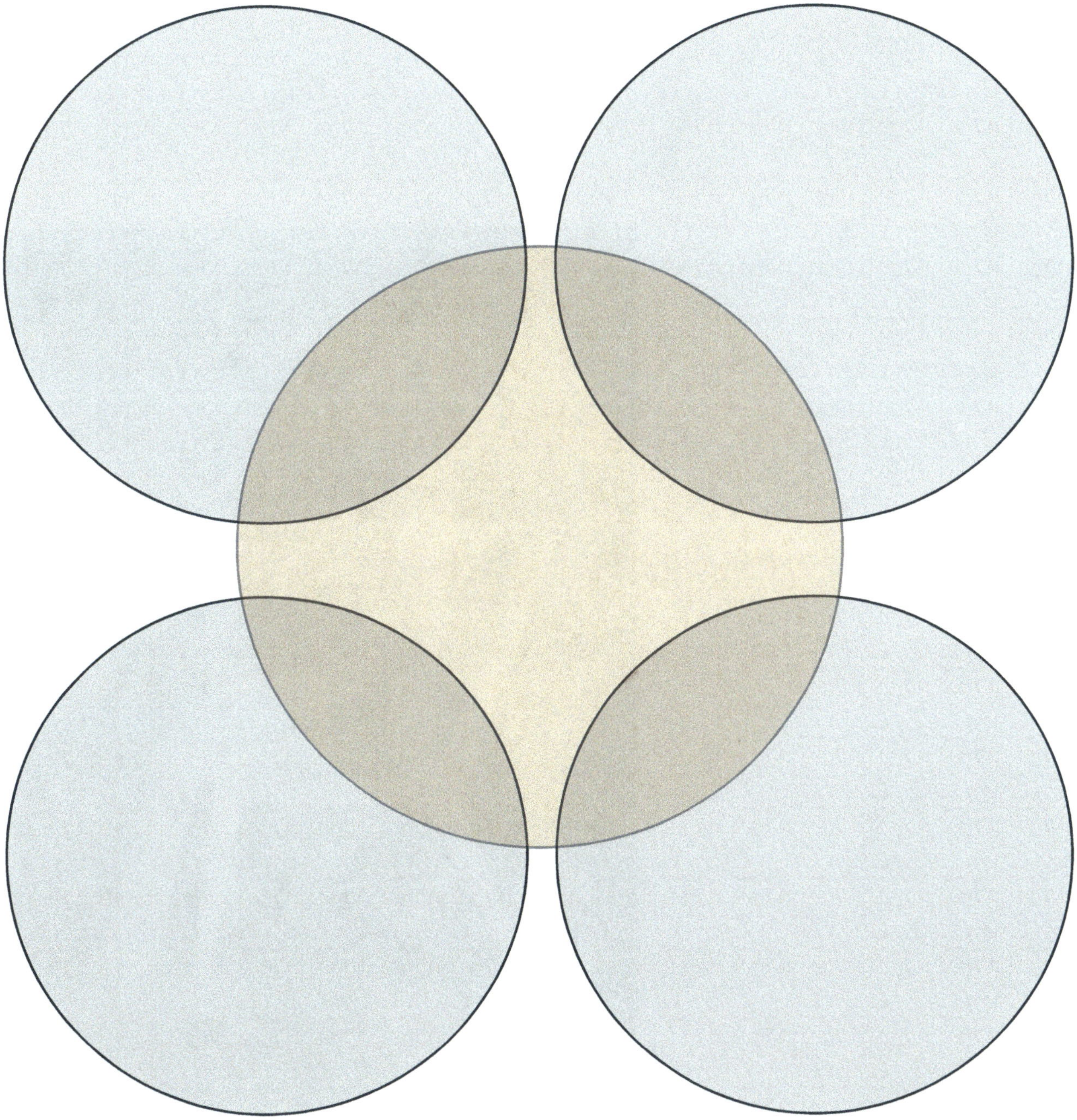

Identity

ACTIVE LISTENING

Pair off into groups of two. Sit directly opposite your discussion partner, knee to knee, and listen to their explanation of their identities.

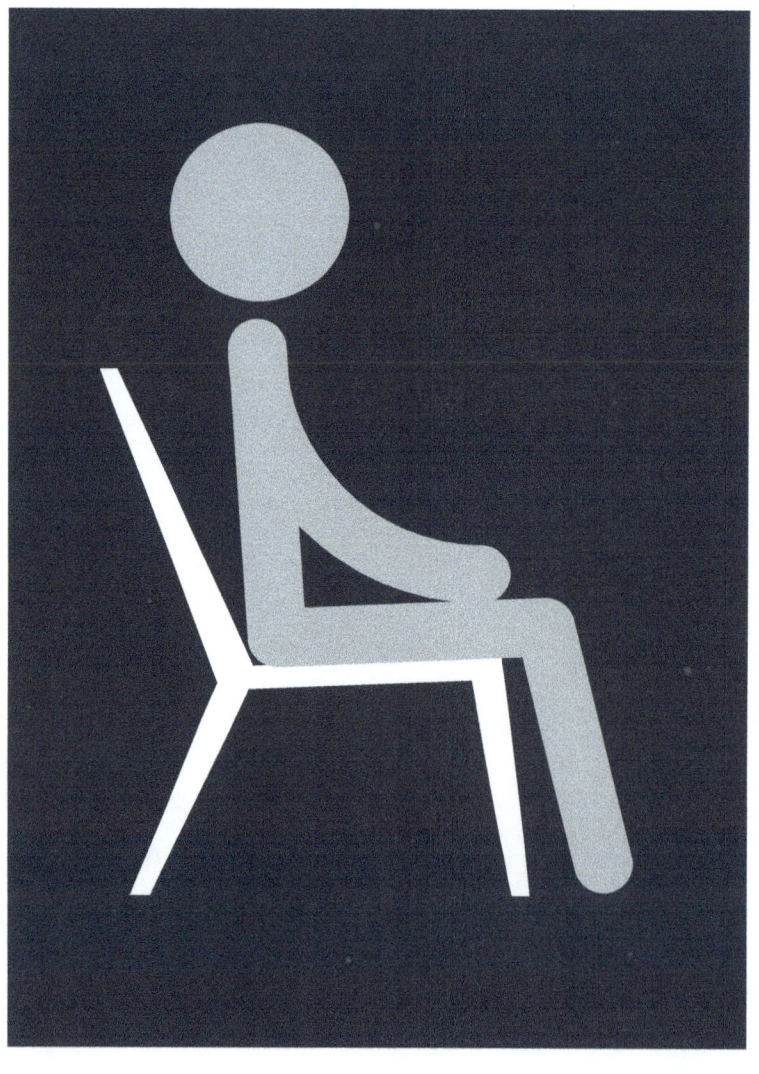

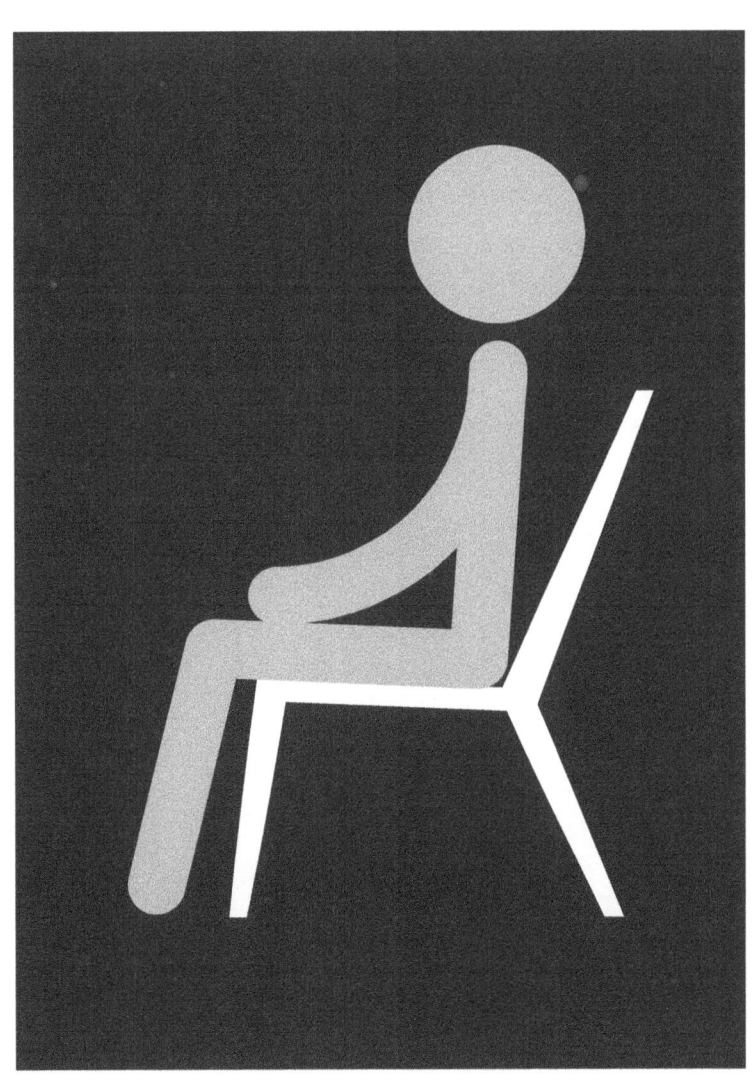

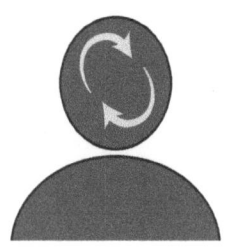

REFLECTION QUESTION

What is happening when you feel heard?

TIMELINE OF EXPERIENCE

Starting with each of the things that have contributed to your socialization, fill in the timeline with important experiences of your life, starting with birth and ending with the present day.

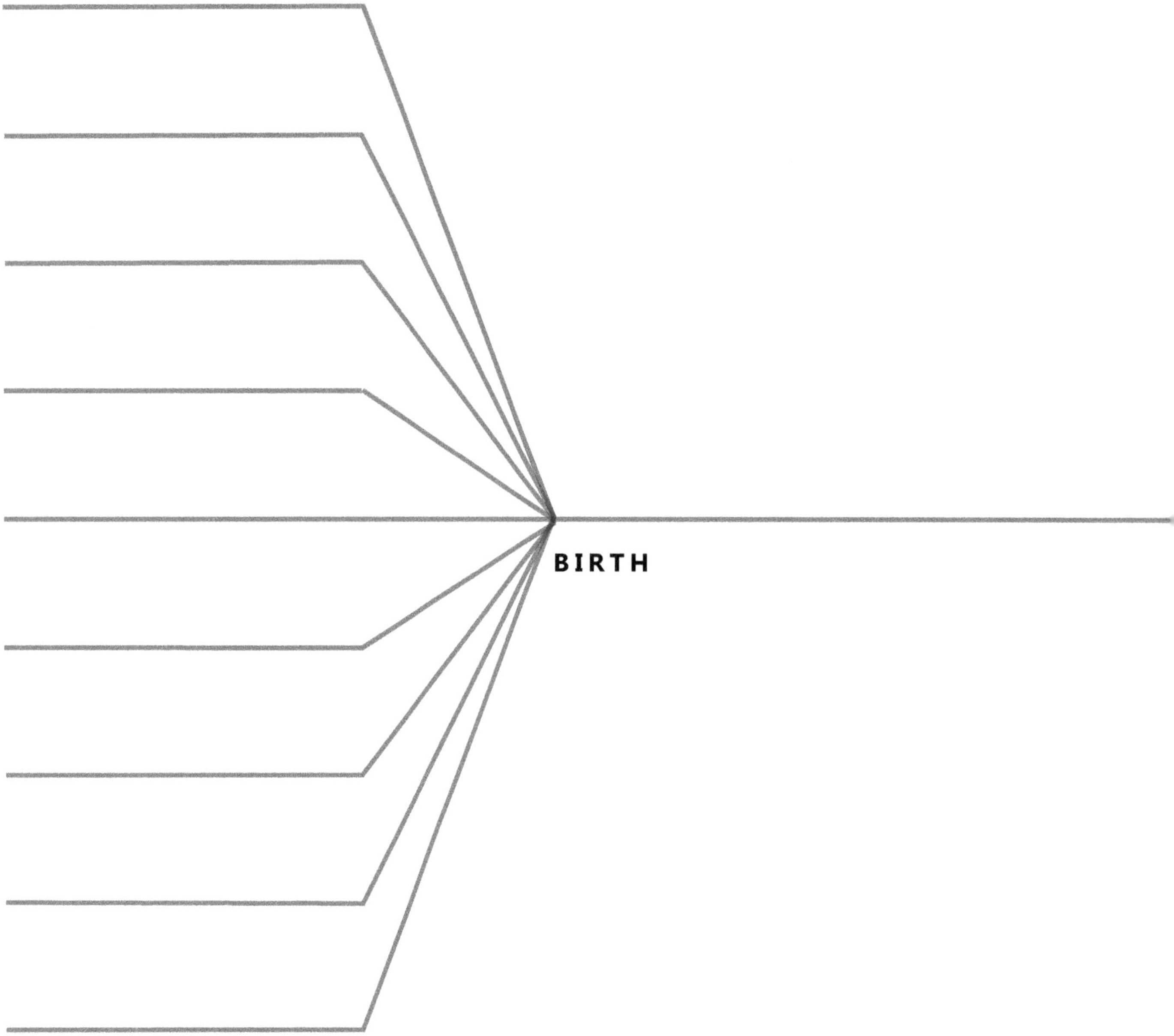

BIRTH

TODAY

TIMELINE ESSAY

List the questions asked by your partner group. Choose one question from your list and then zoom in and get specific. Write about one aspect of your life (at least 2 pages), being as creative as you like. Your response will not be shared with anyone unless you choose to share it.

1.

2.

3.

4.

5.

6.

7.

8.

9.

10.

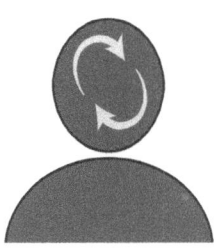

REFLECTION QUESTION

How have your experiences in this circle been different from your experiences in previous circles?

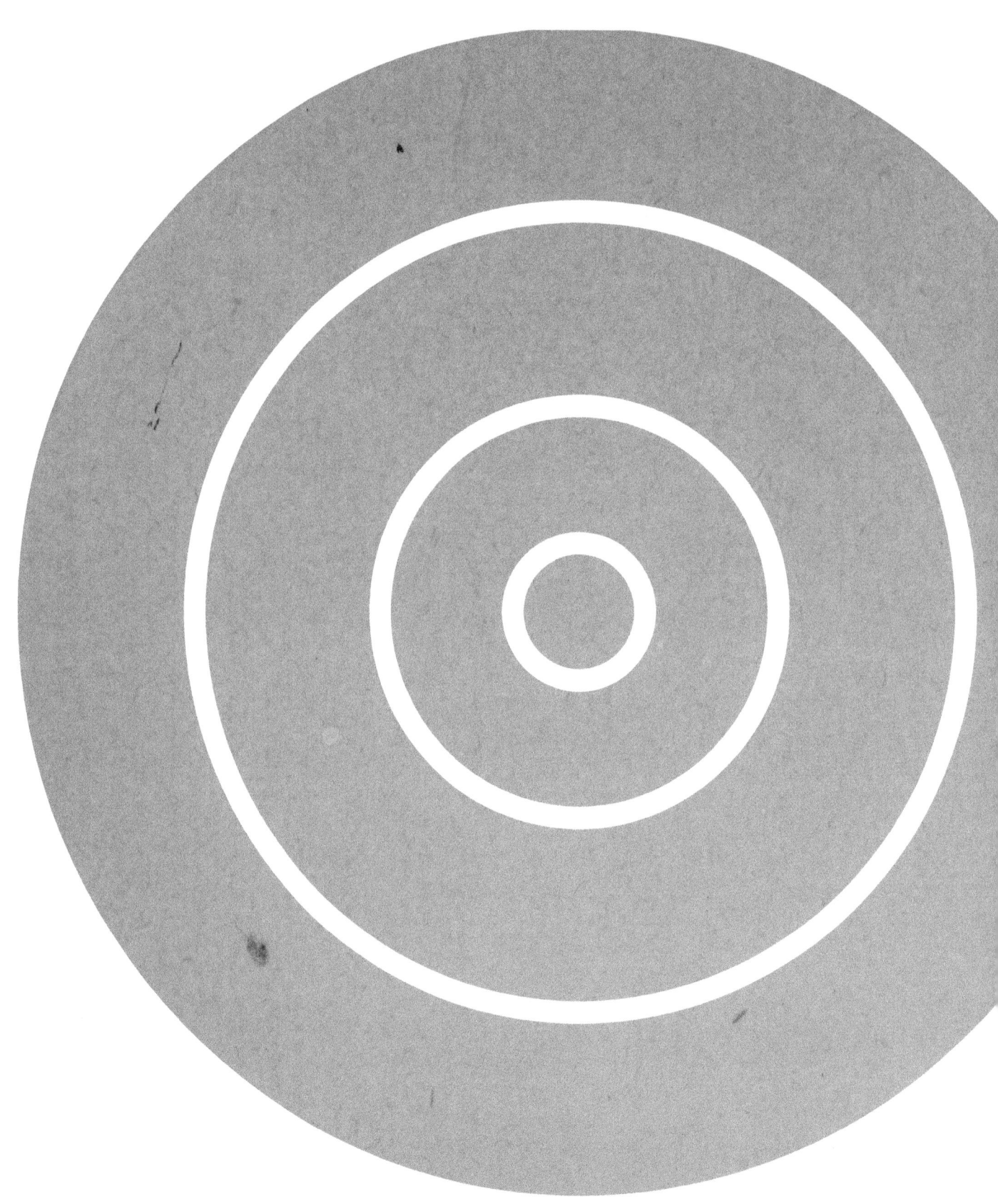

Maggie Wants to Know ... What Are You About?

We are often defined by what we do, as if we are human doings and not human beings. We are asked, "So, what do you do?" And we answer routinely, by rote: "I am an athlete." "I am a musician." "I am a student."

We rarely define ourselves by the things we care about, the things we are *about*. By considering the question "What are you about?" we are able to respond authentically: "I care about being a member of a team." "I care about creating new melodies." "I care about always learning new things."

I had never considered this question until my friend Sally brought it up in a brainstorming session. She expressed that she was tired of being seen only as an athlete. While she was proud to be a student athlete, she wanted to be seen as more than just that. But when we ask people "What do you do?" we reduce the idea of self to the tasks we do and relationships become transactional. We check the boxes: Student, check; Athlete, check; Musician, check.

Sally said that she wanted someone to ask her what she was about, because she cares about so many different things; her sport isn't the only thing that defines her. Sally is people-oriented, someone who cares deeply about her friends and her family. She has a passion for learning and personal growth. She is also an accomplished soccer player.

In that moment Sally discovered something that would take me another two years to realize. I finally made the conscious decision not just to ask "What do you do?" but to hold myself accountable and to go deeper, choosing to be vulnerable by asking myself and others, "What are you about?"

The answer to the question "What are you about?" can change over time, just as people change and grow. Your answer doesn't need to be the same answer every time, but by asking yourself "What am I about?" you challenge yourself to be more present and more honest and intentional. Reflecting on what you are about and answering authentically stops you from just repeating a rote response about what you do with your days or what label is applied to you.

So, what are you about?

What are you passionate about?

What do you care about?

What motivates you to get up in the morning?

When we challenge ourselves to ask new questions, we can move toward a more authentic and intentional awareness of what we are about. We can see ourselves more fully.

In this section you will:

- Develop understanding of identity
- Reflect on the role of intersectionality in community
- Identify the impact of relationship in lived experience
- Experience the role of culture in community
- Explore what it means to operate from a place of curiosity vs. judgment
- Experience and be able to recognize various forms of power

STORY: VISUAL JOURNALING

In the box to the right, define "identity." Then fill these two pages with visual images that tell your story. Who are you in relationship with? How have you been in community before?

Identity is …

INTERSECTIONALITY

Workshop inspired by Kane Smego and CJ Suitt's "The Bridge Project."

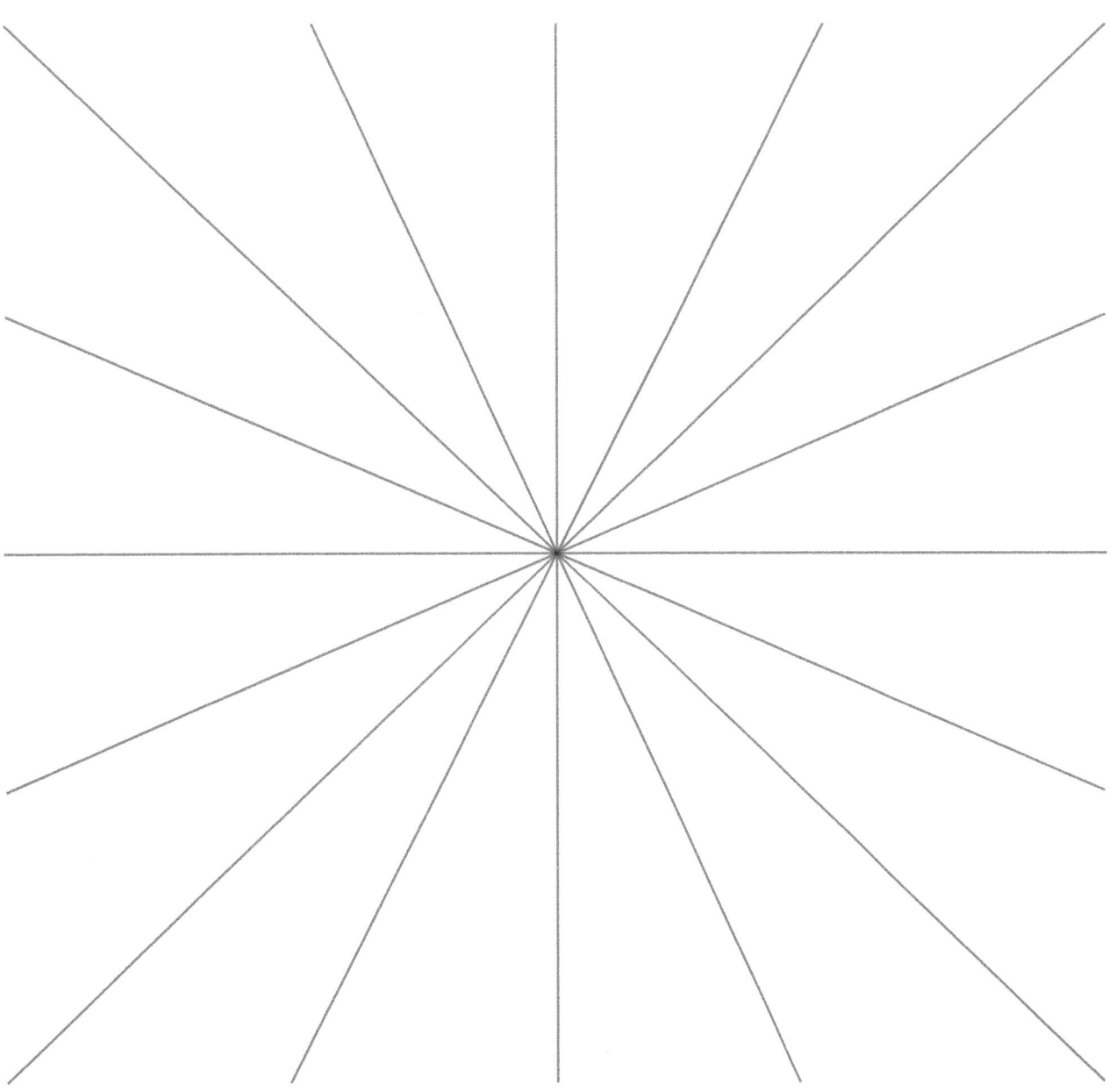

Connection 35

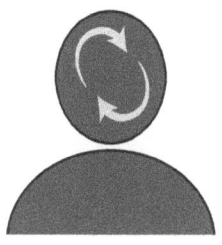

CULTURE SHOCK

Explain a time when you encountered a situation or person whose identities or values seemed different from your own. How might understanding the concept of "intersectionality" have helped you to understand this "culture shock"?

HABITS OF COMMUNITY
What is the culture story of our community?

CURIOSITY VS. JUDGMENT

In this exercise, listen to the scenario presented by your facilitator. Write down details about the scenario and then come up with five questions about it. Do those questions represent curiosity or judgment about the scenario?

SCENARIO	QUESTIONS
	1.
	2.
	3.
	4.
	5.

Interpreting generously means …

RELATIONSHIP MAP

How do you "show up"?

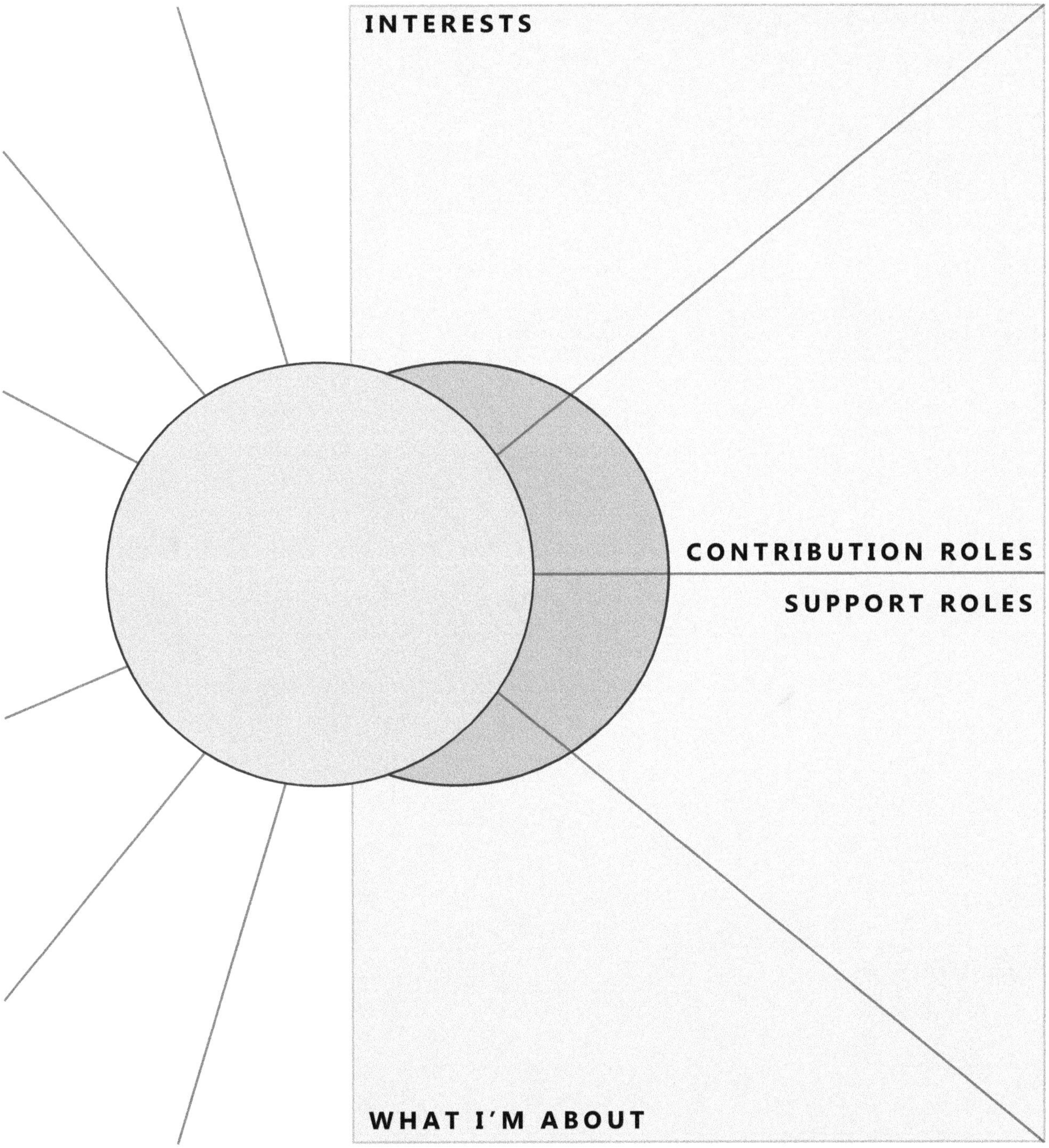

INTERESTS

CONTRIBUTION ROLES

SUPPORT ROLES

WHAT I'M ABOUT

Connection

CONVERSATIONS IN COUNCIL

As we have explored, one of the most important parts of dialogue is listening. This requires actively holding space for others. Who is seated at the rim with you? What do you know about them?

How We Gather …

POWER OVER VS. POWER WITH

Adapted from Lisa VeneKlasen and Valerie Miller, *A New Weave of Power, People & Politics: The Action Guide for Advocacy and Citizen Participation* (2007).

	POWER WITHIN	POWER TO	POWER WITH
INDIVIDUAL	I am unique. I believe that my ideas have value. I recognize my own strengths and abilities and work to expand them. I ask for what I need.	I can contribute. Because of who I am, and the skills that I have practiced, I believe that I have something to offer this community. I offer what I can.	We make a difference. We adhere to the agreements of this community. We value the unique perspectives of others. We are in a generative relationship with one another.
LEADER	Empower	As a leader, I hold space that supports others in the development of skills, knowledge, and disposition, leading to confident ownership of experiences. I provide regular and frequent opportunities for others to engage in meaningful dialogue, thoughtful reflection, and authentic collaboration.	
COMMUNITY	Empowered community	People in this community engage in practices that lead them to care about self, others, and the world they live in. Shared leadership generates a culture of appreciation, inclusion, and wholeness.	

Connection

SILENT COUNCIL

How do you engage with your community? Do you ask others for help? Are you a resource for others? Are you a leader? How do you employ power in your relationships with yourself and others?

NORTH STAR

44   Connection

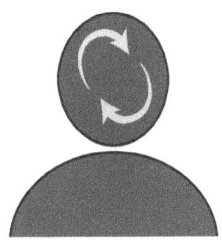

REFLECTION QUESTION

What thoughts or ideas have you come away with from this section?

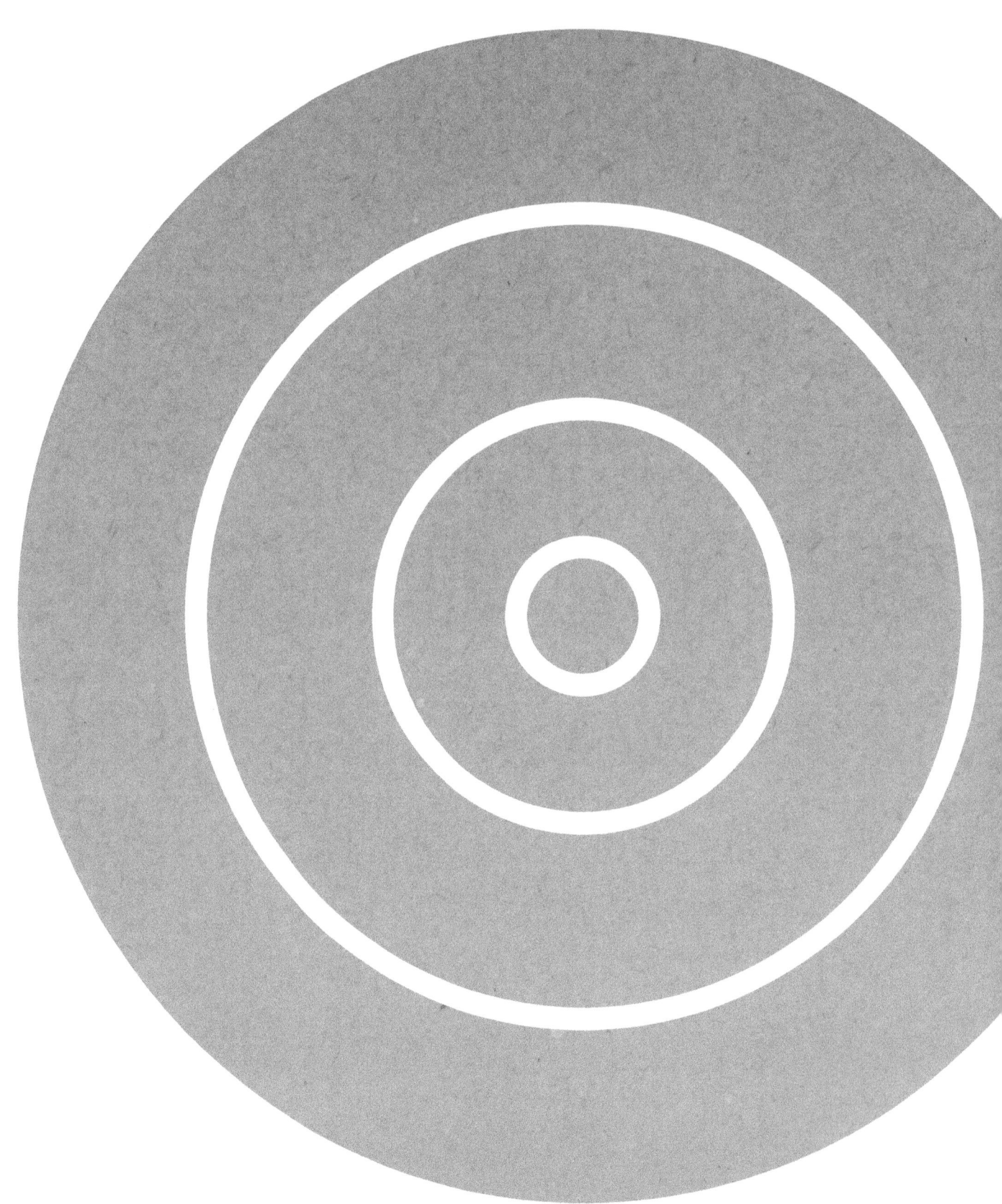

Fire Circles

Remember that story about campground community? Let's come back to that for a minute…

In a time of transition, a small group of us were looking for a way to create community by engaging in dialogue about things that would help construct a more powerful collective. We decided to simply invite people to come together on a particular evening and gather around a fire to talk about our community. Our structure would follow Circle Way guidelines for about an hour, followed by a social time making and consuming the quintessential fireside snack, s'mores!

The questions that we called were equally as simple: *What are the agreements of our community Fire Circle and what is working in this place?* To our delight, we kept having to expand the circle and make room for people to join as we had underestimated the willingness of others to come together in this way. By the time we called that first circle, there were around 35–40 participants. (We didn't know to keep count back then!) The guardian was nervous but warm and welcoming, the keeper was attentive and ensured there was order and space for everyone, and the scribe was kept busy noting key insights that emerged. The diverse group jumped in with both feet, and the sharing was heartfelt, honest, and important. (And the s'mores were delicious!)

From that enthusiastic response, Fire Circles evolved and our core group continued to call a circle every Thursday evening. We kept the process simple: anyone could attend; we called a new question each week; the roles of guardian, keeper, and scribe rotated each week; and every Friday morning our small group came together over breakfast to analyze what showed up the night before to ensure that if there was action to be taken, it would be.

Our small group sustained this practice for a year, and the Fire Circles, in varying forms, continue to burn to this day. That small group of Circle guardians were referred to as *Sparks,* a term that participants lived up to as compassionate leaders, deeply committed to supporting and sustaining their community in positive and powerful ways.

Some of the most important things we learned about engaging in community were learned around those Fire Circles and have been shared throughout this field guide. In the pages that follow, we spiral down into some of the deeper understandings that we believe build and sustain strong communities where everyone is able to thrive.

Creation

In this section you will:

- Strengthen understanding of agreements of community
- Participate in the development of culture within community
- Recognize the power of personal mindset
- Recognize and respond to types of problems
- Experience the ways story impacts personal and collective experiences
- Engage in a dialogic community forum around questions of value

COMMUNITY AGREEMENTS

Agreements establish clear guidelines for individual and collective behavior as we collaborate in the learning. In small groups, use available resources to compare agreements to rules. Prepare to bring your ideas back to the circle.

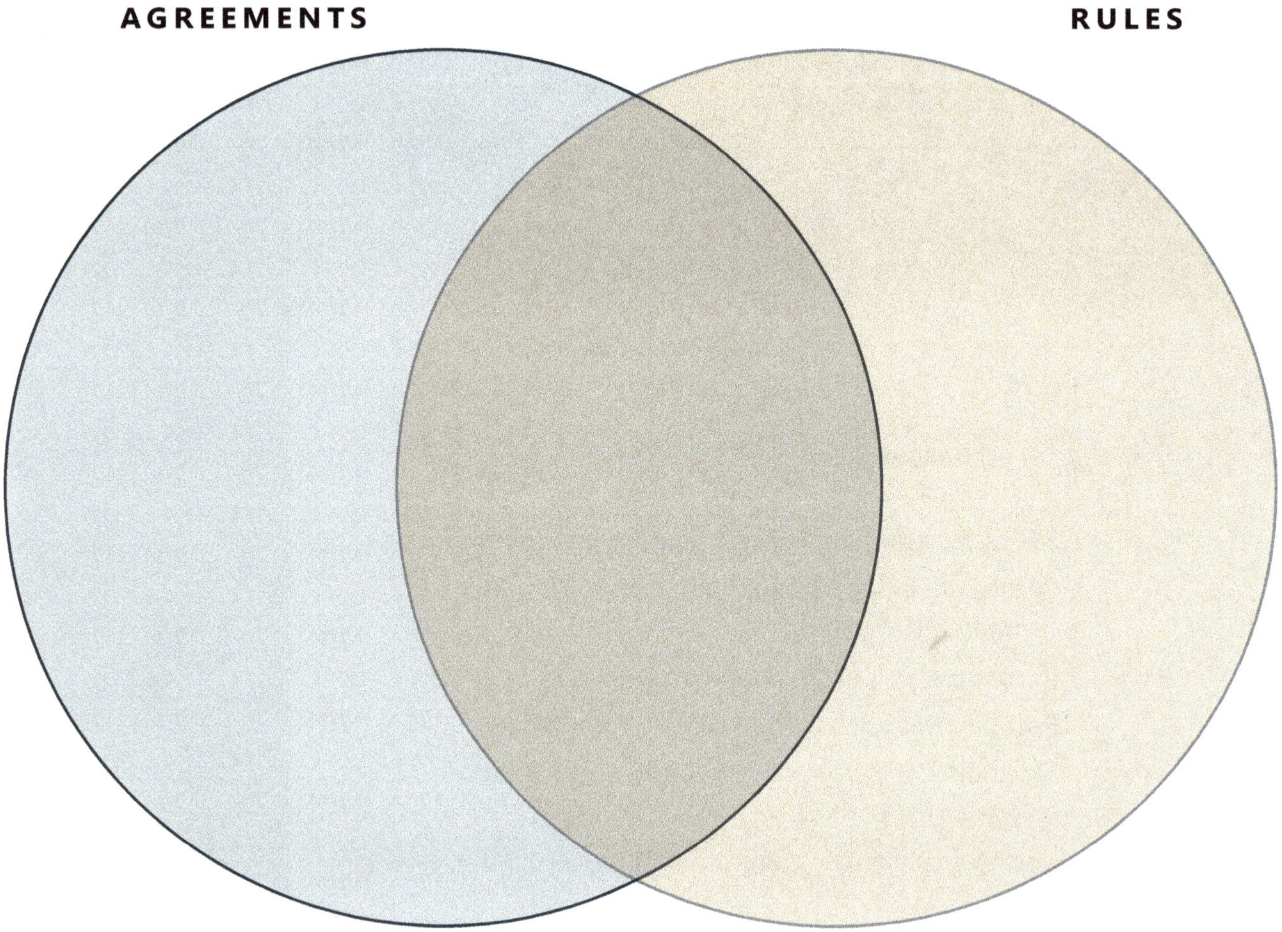

AGREEMENTS **RULES**

COMMUNITY AGREEMENTS

Review the Community Agreements on p. 7. What changes would you suggest?

KEEP THE SAME	CHANGE
1.	1.
2.	2.
3.	3.
4.	4.
5.	5.

The mindset I can adopt to help achieve these community goals is …

YES AND ... FAIL FORWARD

Review the chart below. Then watch the videos and take notes on the facing page.

MINDSET CHARACTERISTICS

From trainugly.com

FIXED		GROWTH
Set You have what you have	**SKILLS & INTELLIGENCE**	Can be grown and developed
How they look Performance focus	**MAIN CONCERN**	Learning, getting better Process focus
Something you do when you're not good	**EFFORT**	An important part of learning
Give up Check out	**CHALLENGES**	Perseverance Work though it
Take it personal Get defensive	**FEEDBACK**	Like it Use it to learn
Hate them Try to avoid making them	**MISTAKE**	Treat them as a learning opportunity

VIDEO 1

VIDEO 2

VIDEO 3

GROWTH MINDSET I

In small groups, discuss how a growth mindset can be useful to individual learners. Use the space below for notes.

GROWTH MINDSET II

In your group, come up with five concrete examples that show how you can implement a growth mindset to succeed. Be prepared to share with the closing circle.

1.

2.

3.

4.

5.

THREE TYPES OF PROBLEMS

FOUR LEVELS OF STORY

Adapted from Alan Seale's *Create a World That Works: Tools for Personal and Global Transformation* (2010).

Creation

 **WORLD CAFE**

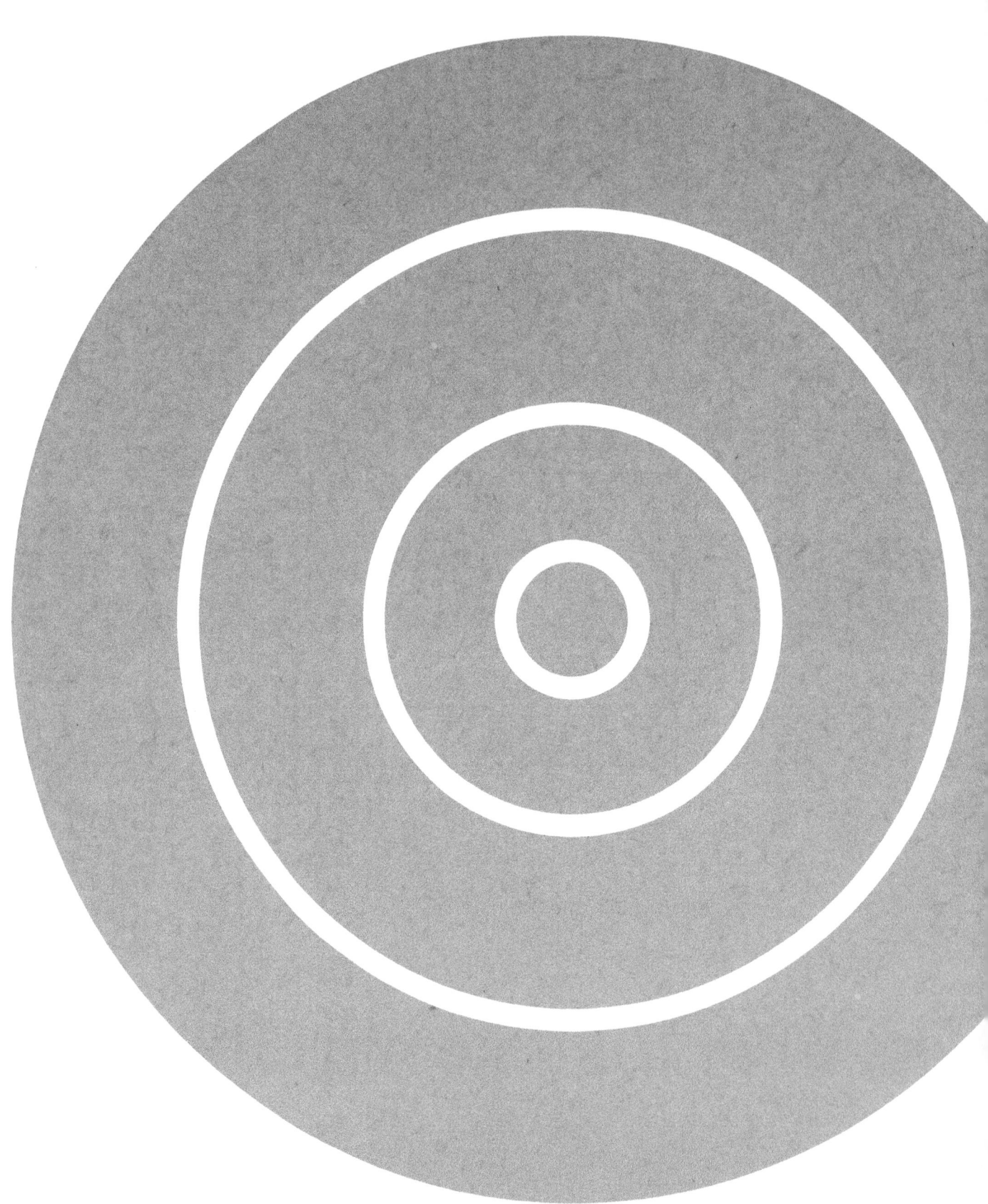

Community of Choice

In the Four Levels of Story, you learned that when you step across the line and recognize that you are operating from a place of *choice,* everything becomes an *opportunity*. Who would you be if you recognized this, your here-and-now place, as your *community of choice?*

Think from that place and take a look at these choice-driven questions to ask yourself:

- What am I about?
- What is mine to do in this place, in the time I have here?
- How will I respond when things get hard?
- What resources will I seek when I need to turn something into an opportunity for growth or change?
- In moments of celebration, what practices can I put into place that honor who I am and what I have accomplished?
- What do I want to add to my timeline?
- How has my relationship circle expanded and how has it expanded me?
- What is the story I want to tell about my experience?

Engagement

In this section you will:

- Determine what your needs are in achieving self-actualization
- Develop a plan for aligning beliefs and actions with personal outcomes
- Reflect on community resources that support success
- State intentions for supporting the success of self and community

HIERARCHY OF NEEDS

Working in small groups, fill in the pyramid below with the levels of human needs.

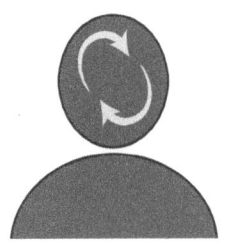

REFLECTION QUESTION

Where are you at? What are your needs right now?

DIRECTION OF INTENTION

In the circle to the right, identify a goal. Then, on the blue line, identify people who will help you reach your goal. On the tan line, identify behaviors that will help you reach your goal. Finally, inside the arrow, identify action steps that will move you toward your goal.

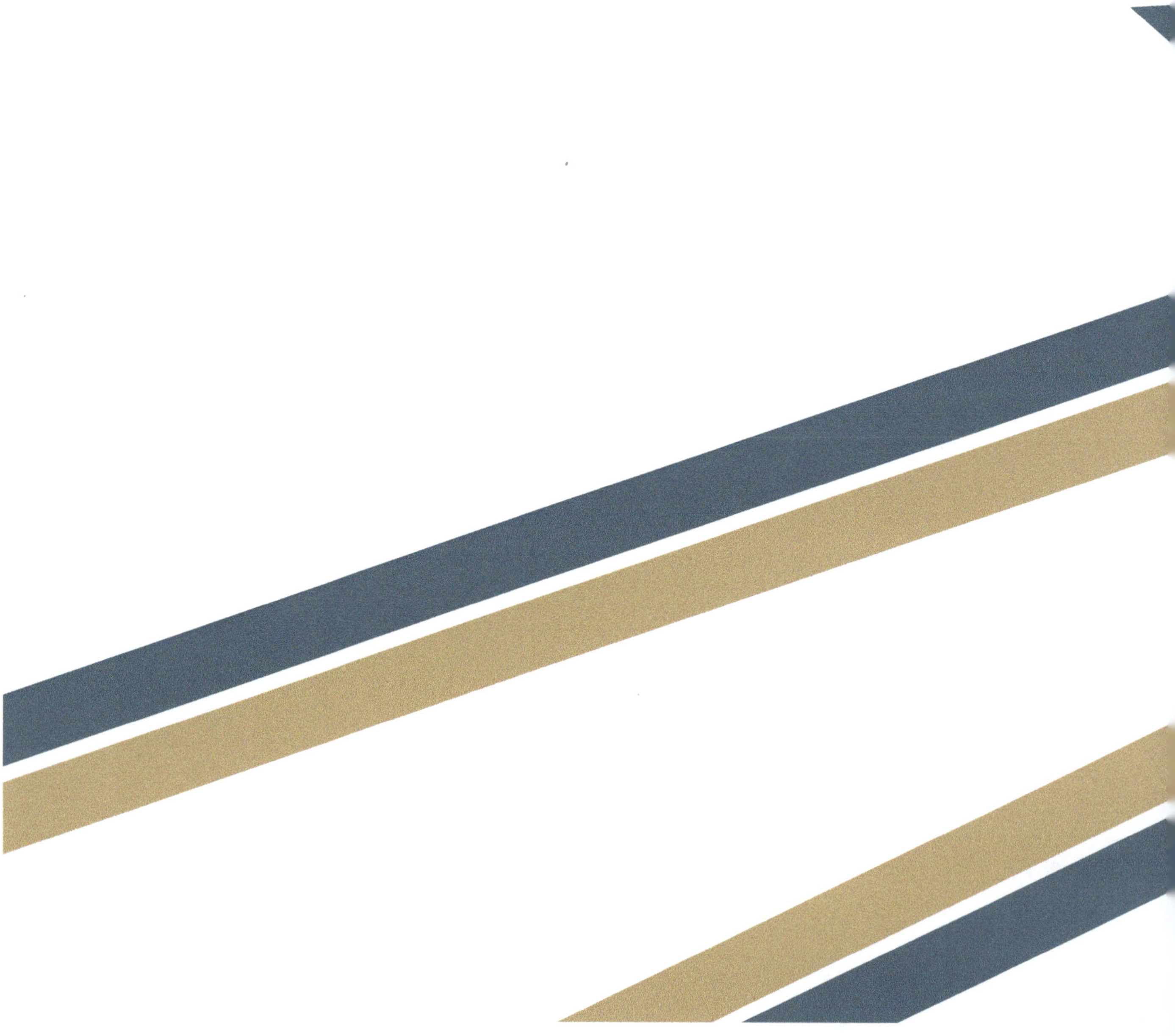

Engagement

RESOURCES
Individually or in small groups, identify the resources you need to succeed. Note contacts, email addresses, etc.

Engagement

TOOLS FOR SUCCESS

Throughout this book you have completed Compass exercises that encourage self-awareness and self-reflection. These exercises, which are indicated with a Compass icon (see left), teach useful skills for life learning.

Using the Kraft paper provided by your facilitator, create a poster that includes all of your completed Compass exercises. You may be as creative as you like ... take pictures, print them out, and paste them on your poster. Redraw each of your exercises. The choice is yours.

Be prepared to share your poster with the group.

TIMELINE OF EXPERIENCE	pp. 22–23
INTERSECTIONALITY	pp. 34–35
SILENT COUNCIL	p. 44
WORLD CAFE	pp. 60–61
DIRECTION OF INTENTION	pp. 68–69
RESOURCES	pp. 70–71

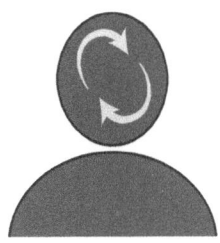

REFLECTION QUESTION

How can your "Tools for Success" poster help you navigate life?

WHAT NOW?

Remember that a field guide is a place to capture what you have observed about your experience. It is a place to return to. Take note of your learning, consider how it might be helpful to return to time and again. This is your book and this is your time. What will you make of it?

www.ingramcontent.com/pod-product-compliance
Lightning Source LLC
Chambersburg PA
CBHW051354110526
44592CB00024B/2983